Ju
296.431
D84   Drucker, Malka.
         Rosh Hashanah and
      Yom Kippur.

Ju
296.431
D84   Drucker, Malka.
         Rosh Hashanah and
      Yom Kippur.

Temple Israel Library
Minneapolis, Minn.

Please sign your full name on the above
card.

Return books promptly to the Library or
Temple Office.

Fines will be charged for overdue books
or for damage or loss of same.

Rosh Hashanah and Yom Kippur

Sweet Beginnings

This man is blowing a shofar.

a JEWISH HOLIDAYS book

ROSH HASHANAH AND YOM KIPPUR
SWEET BEGINNINGS

by Malka Drucker
drawings by Brom Hoban

HOLIDAY HOUSE · NEW YORK

OTHER JEWISH HOLIDAYS BOOKS
Hanukkah: Eight Nights, Eight Lights
Passover: A Season of Freedom

Library of Congress Cataloging in Publication Data

Drucker, Malka.
  Rosh Hashanah and Yom Kippur.

  (A Jewish holidays book)
  Summary: Discusses the meaning of Rosh Hashanah and
Yom Kippur customs. Includes recipes, crafts, puzzles,
and games.
  1. High Holy Days—Juvenile literature. [1. High
Holy Days. 2. Fasts and feasts—Judaism.]   I. Hoban,
Brom.   II. Title.   III. Series: Jewish holidays book.
BM693.H5D78   296.4'31   81-2928
ISBN 0-8234-0427-7   AACR2

ACKNOWLEDGMENTS

THE AUTHOR would like to thank the following people for reading the manuscript and offering helpful suggestions: Rabbi Harold M. Schulweis, Rabbi Lawrence A. Hoffman, Vicky Kelman, Rita Frischer, and Steven Drucker.

She would also like to thank:

Atheneum Publishers for permission to reprint "I'm Sorry" from *The Way Things Are and Other Poems* by Myra Cohn Livingston (A Margaret K. McElderry Book). Copyright © 1974 by Myra Cohn Livingston. Used by permission of Atheneum Publishers.

The Rabbinical Assembly for permission to reprint "This is my Prayer," translation by Norman Tarnor from the Hebrew of Hillel Bavli, and "Kiddush," "She-Heheyanu," "Kol Nidre," and "U-Netanneh Tokef" from the *Mahzor for Rosh Hashanah and Yom Kippur,* edited by Rabbi Jules Harlow. Copyright © 1972 by The Rabbinical Assembly. Reprinted by permission of The Rabbinical Assembly.

ABOUT THE PHOTO CREDITS:

Skirball is short for Hebrew Union College Skirball Museum, Los Angeles.

Yivo is short for "from the archives of the Yivo Institute for Jewish Research."

JTS is short for The Jewish Theological Seminary of America.

For my newborn niece, Chloe,
and her parents, grandparents,
and great-grandparents

CONTENTS

TO THE READER

Rosh Hashanah and Yom Kippur are the holiest and most solemn days of the Jewish year. They are also the most difficult to understand because, unlike other Jewish holidays, they don't celebrate a season or an important historical event. Instead they celebrate something intensely personal and extraordinary—the human being's ability to grow and change. Called the High Holy Days, Rosh Hashanah and Yom Kippur are a time for deep thought, self-examination, and prayer, all of which are hard to do.

Even if you aren't ready to grasp the deepest meaning of these holidays, there are two reasons why it's worthwhile to try to understand them. First, you will see why the High Holy Days are taken so seriously by adults. Second, knowing about the holidays and the awe they inspire will give you a clue to what you may someday feel.

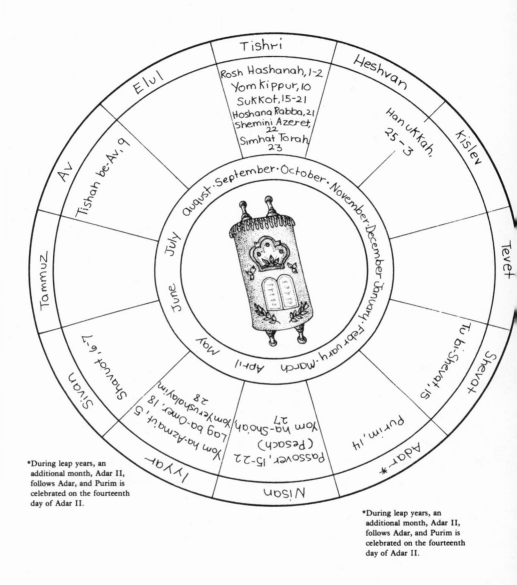

This drawing shows the Jewish calendar in relation to the general (Julian) one.

LINDA HELLER

I
WAKING UP

*Sleepers, awake from your sleep! Slumberers,
rouse yourselves from your slumber! Search
your deeds and do* teshuvah: *remember your
Creator!*

MAIMONIDES, *Hilkhot Teshuvah*

Rosh Hashanah, the first holiday of the Jewish calendar, celebrates the beginning of the world and the creation of man and
woman. It also marks the start of the Jewish year—the first of
Tishri, which coincides with September or early October. It is
the time when summer vacations have ended, school has
started again, and, in many places, the weather has turned
crisp and cool. New classes, new clothes, and new activities
distinguish the season.

Although Rosh Hashanah is the new year, it originally
began as one of four new years. According to one system of
counting the months, it fell in the seventh month of the year.

13

The *Torah*, which is what Jews call the first five books of the Bible, announces the holiday: "In the seventh month, on the first day of the month, you shall observe a sacred occasion: You shall not work when the horn is sounded."

The rabbis offered another reason why the seventh month was chosen to head the year. Seven is a number of wholeness and completion. The seventh day of the week, the Sabbath, is the holiest day of the week because it was the day on which God rested after creating the universe. The seventh month is the holiest month of the year because of Rosh Hashanah's link to creation and birth. Another name for the holiday is *Yom Harat Olam*, birthday of the world.

The Jewish New Year is not like the New Year's holiday that is celebrated on January 1. Instead of throwing parties and using noisemakers, Jews celebrate joyfully but quietly. They look back at the past year to decide which deeds felt right and which deeds did not. Because God is everywhere, even within each human being, self-examination is a way of searching for the part of God inside everyone. The search takes time. There is no sudden revelation of having found something. It doesn't even begin on Rosh Hashanah. It begins in *Elul*, the month before Tishri. This is a month of preparation, but, unlike the other holidays that include cooking, cleaning, or building, the preparation is invisible because it takes place within.

During Elul, many Jews do certain things to help them get into the intensely serious mood of the High Holy Days. In addition to their daily prayers, they recite Psalm 27 because it describes God's relationship to people: "The Lord is my light." Another change in the morning service (except on the Sabbath) is the blowing of the *shofar*, or ram's horn, a 3,000-year-old musical instrument. Rosh Hashanah is also called *Yom*

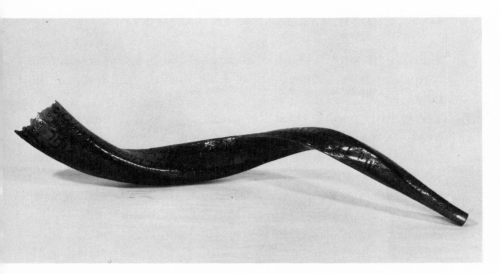

19th-century Sephardic shofar, engraved   THE JEWISH MUSEUM

The outer curve of this European shofar is carved with pierced scallops.   SKIRBALL

Teru'ah, Day of the Shofar. Its urgent blasts help each person to awake from one's daily routine and to prepare for the holiday.

Primitive people used the ram's horn as a noisemaker on New Year's to drive away demons. The Jewish people adapted this custom by blowing the shofar at Rosh Hashanah. They didn't blow the shofar to scare away the demons but to remind the Jewish people to measure and judge their deeds. The shofar is made from the horn of any kosher animal—an animal that chews its cud or has cloven hooves—but the most common shofar is the ram's horn. It is often etched with designs. Eastern European Jews, from whom most American Jews are descended, use a small shofar, about twelve inches long, that is curved upward. This is so that its sounds and one's prayers go upward to heaven. The Sephardic Jews, who are from the Middle East and Mediterranean countries, use a longer, fancier, and more elaborate long shofar with two or three twists in it. Generally the smaller shofar has a better sound.

Despite its remarkable sound, the shofar is made simply. A horn is boiled in water until it is soft. Then it is hollowed out on the inside and the wider end is slightly flattened. The mouth piece is then shaped and the shofar is put aside to harden.

The sound of the shofar is clear and loud. At one time, it heralded great events. It summoned armies to battle, proclaimed a new king, and announced the Sabbath and festivals. In modern times, the shofar was blown at the Western Wall in Jerusalem when the Old City was liberated and the whole city of Jerusalem was reunited. Although it is used only occasionally for such grand moments, the shofar still holds a special place in Jewish ceremony. It seems to express feelings that cannot be put into words: feelings of wanting to change and

STEPHANIE SABAR

This child is blowing a Sephardic shofar.

This is a New Year's card of a mother blessing her child on Yom Kippur eve. SKIRBALL

being excited by the chance to do so, but also of being afraid of changing. Like a baby's cry that proclaims new life, the shofar may be the cry of the new self that is born in everyone on Rosh Hashanah.

Maimonides, one of the wisest philosophers of the Middle Ages, believed the shofar said, "Wake up! Rosh Hashanah is coming! Think! What did you do last year? Decide what to do next year." The shofar has three sounds. The first is called *teki'ah*. It is a long, clear blast. The second sound is *shevarim*, three short blasts. The third sound is *teru'ah*, nine very fast short notes. The last sound is *teki'ah gedolah*, the "great blast." The blower of the shofar holds this note as long as possible.

The amazing thing about these sounds is that there is nothing inside the shofar to make the sounds. It is absolutely hollow. The word *shofar* comes from a root word that means "hollow" in Hebrew. The shofar is an empty instrument that becomes special only with a person's breath in it. It takes a human being to make it holy.

The person who is chosen to blow the shofar for Rosh Hashanah and Yom Kippur is called the *ba'al teki'ah*, the master of the shofar. It's a great honor to be asked to blow the shofar before the congregation, and the ba'al teki'ah practices every day during Elul. When the time comes for the shofar to be blown, there are feelings of nervousness throughout the congregation. The ba'al teki'ah is blowing for everyone, and if there is a mistake, it is shared by all listening.

Elul is also the month when people send New Year cards to one another. The greeting in these cards is rarely "Happy New Year." Instead it is usually *"Le-Shanah Tovah Tikkatevu,"* or "May You Be Inscribed for a Good Year." The message implies that a year of good deeds will be a happy one. Elul is the month to visit the graves of relatives and other loved ones. Remembering the dead is connected with the idea of birth. All living things die, but memory gives them new life.

In the nineteenth century, the anticipation in Eastern Europe before the High Holy Days was great. Children looked forward to the season almost as much as adults because the days from the middle of Elul until after *Sukkot*, the fall harvest festival which follows Rosh Hashanah, were vacation days from school. Still, children sensed an air of seriousness that dampened their freedom. They busied themselves by gathering little "Elul pears" in the forest. These were eaten all winter on Friday nights after the Sabbath meal.

During Elul, the *shammash*, or caretaker of the synagogue, awakened each Jewish family before dawn for early-morning *selihot* prayers. The selihot are special prayers to prepare one for the High Holy Days. The rabbis thought that God hovered closest in the early morning hours. The shammash knocked on doors and windows with a shofar-shaped hammer to awaken the members of the family. He would say, "Be strong as a leopard, swift as an eagle, fleet as a deer, and mighty as a lion to do the will of your Heavenly Creator." Occasionally a non-Jewish family would ask the shammash to awaken them because they believed that early awakening would bring them luck.

Jews no longer awaken before dawn to say selihot prayers during Elul, but they do begin saying them the Saturday night before Rosh Hashanah if it is at least four days from the holiday. If it is fewer than four days, they begin the week before, saying the prayers while it is still dark. Since the prayers can be said anytime after midnight, many synagogues hold a special midnight service on Saturday night to begin the High

Holy Day season. Here is a poem for selihot, recited in a modern service:

This is my prayer to You, O my God:
Let me not swerve from my life's path,
Let not my spirit wither and shrivel
In its thirst for You
And lose the dew
With which You sprinkled it
When I was young.

Be my heart open
To every broken thing,
To orphaned life,
To every stumbler
Wandering unknown
And groping in the shadow.

Rosh Hashanah is celebrated for two days by Conservative and Orthodox Jews, one day by Reform Jews. The fact that it is two days long stresses its importance, but it also lasts two days because the Jewish calendar is a lunisolar calendar. The moon (lunar) determines the months, and the sun (solar) determines the year. The months are as long as the moon's cycle, which is twenty-nine and a half days. Each new moon is a small holiday called *Rosh Hodesh,* Head of the Month. The first of Tishri is a new moon. In ancient times, the rabbis could not predict exactly when the new moon would occur, so they extended the new year to two days to be sure that Rosh Hashanah would be celebrated at the right time.

The holiday starts at sundown, as do all Jewish holidays, and it begins at home. The table is set with a white tablecloth because the color for the High Holy Days is white. It is a color of freshness, newness, simplicity, and purity. The holiday has a warm and bright beginning—the lighting and blessing of two candles (see Appendix).

After the candle lighting, the *She-Heheyanu*, the prayer of thanksgiving, is said: "Praised are You, Lord our God, King of the universe, for granting us life, for sustaining us, and for helping us reach this day." A cup of sweet wine is poured, and the *kiddush*, the prayer blessing the holiday, is recited (see Appendix). Then the *ha-motzi*, the blessing over the food, is said. The candle lighting, kiddush, and the ha-motzi are part of every major Jewish holiday.

A mother is photographing her family, which is gathered around the holiday table.   YIVO

These three children enjoy the sweet taste of apples dipped in honey.
STEPHANIE SABAR

Two things make the meal on Rosh Hashanah eve different from other holiday meals. First, the *hallah*, the holiday bread, is an unusual shape. The hallah for festivals and the Sabbath is a long, oval braided bread. On Rosh Hashanah the hallah resembles a crown, since Rosh Hashanah is the "head" of the year. Sometimes the Rosh Hashanah hallah is shaped like a ladder, which stands for the connection between life on earth and the heavens. Some say the prayers travel up the ladder to God. The hallah is dipped in honey and eaten.

The second difference is that an apple is cut into pieces and dipped in honey. After this is done, everyone at the table says: "Praised are You, Heavenly One, Ruler of the universe, who creates the fruit of the tree." After the apple is eaten, everyone says: "May it be Your will, God and God of our fathers and mothers, to renew on us a good and sweet year." The custom is to serve nothing sour or bitter for the season. The hope is that sweetness will last for the whole year. Some people also place on the table a cooked whole fish, head included, because a head represents leadership and greatness.

In Israel, Jews who live on *kibbutzim*—communities where people work, live, and eat together—celebrate the holidays together, too. On Rosh Hashanah evening, the children act as "messengers of good deeds" and distribute wine, pomegranates, honey, and gifts. The dining hall is decorated with symbols of the holiday. One of the symbols is the zodiac sign for Tishri, a set of scales. The scales are a reminder of the weighing of good and bad deeds.

Rosh Hashanah is also called *Yom ha-Din*, Day of Judgment. Judging one's deeds goes on all year, but during the forty-day period from the first of Elul to Yom Kippur, the Jewish people do this together. The combined energy of a community gives strength and comfort to the individual, just as a team does to an individual player whose energy is flagging. The other reason for praying together is that each Jew strengthens or weakens the community by his or her deeds. Each good deed helps the Jewish people; each wrongdoing weakens it.

In the morning the family goes to the synagogue. If there is only one time during the year that a Jew goes to synagogue, it will probably be during the High Holy Days. The intensity of the season is a magnet that pulls people into the synagogue and into themselves. Everyone brings or is given a *mahzor*, the special High Holy Day prayer book that is filled with prayers, songs, and ideas connected with examining the direction of one's life. Many of the prayers are rhymes or acrostics because, before the existence of prayer books, acrostics helped people to memorize the prayers. The people in the synagogue greet one another with *"Le-Shanah Tovah"*—"May you have a good year!"

The service lasts all morning. The recited parts of the Torah are about children. The first portion tells the story of how much Sarah and Abraham wanted a child, but did not conceive one until they were very old. The child was Isaac. The second portion tells about how Hannah was blessed with her

The relief representation on the spine of this 18th-century Dutch mahzor is of King David with his harp.   THE JEWISH MUSEUM

18th-century tapestry of Hannah and Samuel
THE METROPOLITAN MUSEUM OF ART, GIFT OF JULIA A. BERWIND, 1953

son, Samuel, also after years of barrenness. Children are central to the High Holy Days because they are the link between past and future; they are the new start of every generation.

The best-known High Holy Day prayer is the *U-Netanneh Tokef* (see Appendix), which is read during the morning service. It asks: Who shall be rich in the year to come and who shall be poor? Who shall live and who shall die? Perhaps these words should not be taken literally. Rather, they should be understood as general questions about who shall be part of life and who shall remain asleep, bored, and discontent with life. U-Netanneh Tokef is also a prayer of ecology. If you poison the air and water with machines, you shall die. Like all the holiday prayers, it encourages people to choose to live by doing good deeds and being open and caring to others. The mahzor reminds people of their choice: "I call heaven and earth to witness against you this day: I have put before you life and death, blessing and curse. Choose life." The prayer ends: "But *tefillah, teshuvah,* and *tzedakah* will avoid the severe decree." *Tefillah* means "prayer," and *teshuvah* means "to return." *Tzedakah* means "justice," which is giving to those in need.

The shofar is blown after the Torah readings. It is blown three more times during the service to equal one hundred notes. Sometimes the ba'al teki'ah will hide the shofar in his *tallit,* or prayer shawl, until it is time to blow it. Then he will remove the shofar and cover his head with the tallit. This adds to the awesomeness and majesty of the day.

After the service, the family returns home for a small festive meal, again with hallah, fruit, and honey. In the afternoon, Orthodox Jews go to a nearby stream, river, or ocean for *tashlikh,* the casting away of sins. It's an old custom that helps to express the feeling of emptying oneself and starting cleanly. Everyone's pockets are filled with bread crumbs, which symbolize the sins of the old year. When people reach the water, they turn their pockets inside out and say, "You will cast all the sins of your people, the house of Israel, into a place where they shall be no more remembered or visited or even come to mind." If there is no water nearby, they go to a well or a high peak that overlooks the water.

The Hasidim, fervent Jews from Eastern Europe, used to perform tashlikh at nightfall by the light of candles. After they shook themselves free of crumbs, they took candles and lit small bundles of straw. They put these "little boats" in the water. The Hasidim were joyous because they believed the water swept away their sins and the fires burned them.

On the next day of Rosh Hashanah, the story of the binding of Isaac is read from the Torah in the synagogue. God told Abraham to sacrifice his favorite son, Isaac, on Mount Moriah. Although Abraham loved Isaac very much, he was ready to sacrifice him to demonstrate his love and faith to God. Early in the morning, he took Isaac far from home. When Isaac saw the wood, the knife, and the stone to ignite the wood, he asked his father, "Here are the firestone and the wood; but where is the sheep for the burnt offering?"

Abraham answered, "God will see to the sheep for His burnt offering."

When they arrived at Mount Moriah, Abraham built an altar. He laid the wood for the fire, tied up Isaac, and laid him on the altar on top of the wood. Isaac was frightened, but dared not say a word. Just as his father trusted God, so he trusted his father. Suddenly the angel of God told Abraham not to hurt his son. Abraham looked up and saw a ram caught

A modern tashlikh ceremony   BILL ARON

"Abraham's Sacrifice," an etching by Rembrandt

in a bush. He sacrificed the ram instead of Isaac, and that is why the ram's horn is the preferred horn for the shofar.

The Torah reading is a reminder that the child is holy, a creation of God. Not only must parents not kill their children, but they also may not force a child to live their dreams. Rosh Hashanah and Yom Kippur are about choice and change. Every person of whatever age has the right to choose his or her own way.

This Torah has a special covering for Rosh Hashanah. BILL ARON

2
TAKING AIM

*Seek the Almighty while He may be found,
call upon Him while He is near.*

ISAIAH

Rosh Hashanah and Yom Kippur are ten days apart. The days between are called *Yamim Nora'im*, the Days of Awe, or *Aseret Yemei Teshuvah*, the Ten Days of Teshuvah. These are tender and delicate days, when people look at the year that has passed and face up to their mistakes, errors in judgment, or wrongdoings. These words are perhaps more appropriate to use than the word *sin*, since it suggests judgment. The Hebrew word for sin means "missing the mark." The guide to finding the mark is the Torah. The *mitzvot*, or commandments for living that are described in the Torah, point to righteousness.

Suppose you want something, but you go about getting it in the wrong way. You've missed the mark. But it's not the end of the world because, if you're able to use the mistake correctly, you'll be able to aim better the next time. If you miss the mark,

33

you can correct it and learn. Mistakes in the Jewish tradition are seen as part of growing and learning.

There is a *midrash*, or legend, about Moses, the great Jewish leader, and his mistake. When Moses came down from Mount Sinai with the Ten Commandments engraved upon two stone tablets, he saw the Jewish people worshipping a golden calf, an idol, which the men had made from melting their women's jewelry. Moses was enraged, and in his anger he dropped the Ten Commandments.

God told Moses to go into a cave for forty days to make a new set of tablets. When he was finished, he was to put the new tablets into a holy ark or cabinet, along with the pieces he had angrily broken. The broken pieces were to be included to show that they should be treasured as much as the perfect set. From his mistake, Moses had learned that his anger was destructive.

If you've made a mistake, you can do something to correct it. Maimonides, the great medieval philosopher mentioned earlier, describes three steps to teshuvah. First you think of what you've done. The next step is to apologize. The last step answers the question "How do I know that I've done teshuvah, that I've really changed?" The answer is that you don't make the same mistake again. Only after you've completed these steps can you ask forgiveness of God.

Prayer by itself is not holy. It's what the prayer moves you to do that's holy. The importance of the deed is illustrated in "If Not Higher," a story by the Yiddish writer I. L. Peretz. It's about a Hasidic rabbi who was watched carefully by his followers and his doubters during selihot. The doubters wanted to know what he did before he came to the synagogue for morning prayers. His followers believed that he went to heaven to plead for his people.

One doubter decided to find out once and for all where the

"Moses and the Ten Commandments" by Shulamith W. Miller

rabbi went. He secretly followed him home, slept under his bed, and watched him awaken and say his morning prayers. Then the rabbi put on peasant's clothes. What is the rabbi doing? the doubter wondered. Taking an ax, the rabbi went to the woods, chopped some wood, and carried it to an old woman's door. The surprised doubter watched as the rabbi entered her freezing cottage, posing as a woodcutter, and laid a fire for her. He told her that he would collect the money next time. When the doubter returned, everyone asked him eagerly, "Where was he? Did he go to heaven?"

The doubter, who no longer doubted the rabbi's goodness, shook his head and answered softly, "If not higher."

The process of looking within, facing one's mistake, and doing what is necessary to "hit the mark" is called teshuvah, or repentance. The root word is *shuvah,* which means turning, turning from the wrong direction to the right one. The word *repentance* suggests pain, but the pain is like the pain you feel when you exercise to strengthen your body. It's a good pain, not the pain of punishment. The discomfort comes from knowing that you can't fool yourself. You know when you've done something wrong willfully, and there's no escape.

The ten days between Rosh Hashanah and Yom Kippur are a time to forgive and to ask forgiveness from friends and family. To forgive is hard, but to ask forgiveness is even harder. This poem captures both the difficulty and the relief that come from saying you're sorry:

I'M SORRY
by Myra Cohn Livingston

To try to say it,
To put it into words,
To make it come out of my mouth
*   happens slowly.*

THERE

I have said it.
Only one small say:
But it is said.

The person who goes through teshuvah is called *ba'al
teshuvah,* master of the return. The name suggests a respect
for the strength it takes to admit a mistake and the effort it
takes to change. A person who simply begs forgiveness and
pleads weakness is not a master. Changing requires strength.
Forgiving and asking forgiveness, if done sincerely, help you
to change what you've done the year before so as to give birth
to a new self. Of course, you will still be yourself, but you may
discover that you can do things you never thought possible. At
the beginning of the ten Days of Awe, the moon is scarcely
visible. But by Yom Kippur it shines brightly, and the rabbis
said that teshuvah is responsible for its light.

The rabbis also said that teshuvah is necessary to everyone
—the most righteous and the most evil. This is because no one
stays the same. People either go higher or lower during the ten
days. Each person can choose the direction he or she will go,
but the goal is not to be perfect. The person who has done
teshuvah is kinder and more caring, and that is better than
perfection.

The person who has never done wrong is not as holy as the
person who has turned from a wrong deed and made it good.
This is not to say there is no harm in wrongdoing. Rather, it is
like a small child hammering nails into a piece of wood. The
child drives in many of the nails crookedly and begins to cry.
Someone removes the nails so that the child can begin again.
If too many nails have to be taken out, the piece of wood is so
full of holes that there is no room for the good nails anymore.

When people decide to change, they believe that God will

A man praying in his tallit   PHOTO BY IRVING I. HERZBERG

help them to face a new year with renewed energy, hope, and confidence. Life is a partnership between oneself and God. The rabbis explained the relationship between human beings and God by describing a child who has wandered into a forest and gotten lost. When the child's father finds out that the child is lost, he sends this message: Just go as far as you can, and I will meet you the rest of the way.

Sometimes it is the heart, not the head, that will lead the way. It is not the most learned, but the most caring person who will experience teshuvah. A Hasidic tale tells of a small shepherd boy who goes to synagogue with his father. As the boy hears the prayers, he becomes so moved that he wants to pray, but he is ignorant and doesn't know a single word of Hebrew. Suddenly he takes a flute from his pocket and plays a sweet melody to God. The members of the congregation and the boy's father become angry with the boy and tell him to leave. But the rabbi stops them and says, "No, let him stay. All day I've been praying for the gates of heaven to open. That boy's music from his heart has finally moved the gates."

Teshuvah is not overwhelming if it is experienced every year. Even if you've been asleep all year, it's only one year you're accounting for, not your whole life. An artist creates a masterpiece bit by bit—one stroke at a time, one note at a time, one word at a time. It's the same thing with the creation of a new self. It's done day by day, year by year, deed by deed.

There is a special Sabbath that falls between Rosh Hashanah and Yom Kippur, *Shabbat Shuvah*, the Sabbath of Return. It is called that because a portion of the Prophets is read that proclaims, "Return O Israel, unto the Lord thy God." This Sabbath stresses a return to the teachings of the Torah, the path of righteousness. It was also one of the two times of

Early 18th-century plate for the High Holy Days from Delft, Holland

the year in Eastern Europe when the rabbi gave a sermon.

The sermon is a reminder that there is still time to wake up and discover one's strengths. You can let other people judge you and tell you who you are, or you can wake up and decide for yourself. Your good deeds and bad deeds are not written down. They are inside you. You will be your own judge, accountant, and doctor, and you can heal yourself with tefillah, teshuvah, and tzedakah.

Getting ready for kapparot   PHOTO BY IRVING I. HERZBERG

3
A FRESh START

Happy the people who know the trumpet
sound; these walk, O Lord, in the light of Your
face.

PSALMS 89:15

Beginning is the key word for the High Holy Days and in
Jewish thought. The climax to beginning again is Yom Kippur,
the last day of the High Holy Days. Although it's usually
translated as the Day of Atonement, Yom Kippur literally
means the Day of Cleansing or Purification. Jews do not eat,
work, or go to school on Yom Kippur. The day is spent
studying and praying in the synagogue.

The day before Yom Kippur is a small festival, full of anticipation and excitement. Teshuvah has been done, tzedakah
has been given, and the community looks forward to the
holiday. Some Jews practice *kapparot*, an ancient custom in
which the desire to purge oneself of wrongdoings by passing
them to another living thing is acted out symbolically. The

day before Yom Kippur, a live chicken is held over a person's head while he or she says these words: "This is my redemption. This cock (or hen, if the person is female) is going to be killed and I shall enter upon a long, happy and peaceful life." The chicken is a substitute for the person in the ceremony. The chicken is slaughtered and eaten by the family during the meal before Yom Kippur. Sometimes the chicken is given to the poor. Instead of a chicken, eighteen dollars or eighteen coins can be used, because eighteen is the number in Hebrew that means "life." Kapparot may be connected with the animal sacrifices practiced in the time of the Temple. A goat was sacrificed on Yom Kippur for the sins of the community. When the second Temple was destroyed, prayers and good deeds replaced the sacrifices.

In Eastern Europe, kapparot sometimes took a different form. Parents braided baskets for their children fifteen days before Rosh Hashanah and filled the baskets with soil sowed with wheat, barley, beans, and peas. By Rosh Hashanah the plants had grown six inches. Each child took a basket on the eve of Rosh Hashanah, swung it over his or her head seven times, and said, "This is instead of me, this is my exchange." After the ceremony, the children threw the baskets into a stream.

There is a feast in the late afternoon just before the eve of Yom Kippur because the holiday, despite its solemnity, is joyful. It is the day Jews are at peace with God and with themselves. The rabbis said that eating on the day before Yom Kippur is as holy an act as fasting is on Yom Kippur. Jewish festivals alternate fast and feast days because no one knows whether fasting or feasting will bring the Messiah sooner. So people do both.

The hallah for this pre–Yom Kippur feast is sometimes a

Holding a chicken over the heads of two girls during kapparot

PHOTO BY IRVING I. HERZBERG

different shape from Rosh Hashanah hallah. Besides looking like a ladder or crown, it can be shaped like wings to help one's prayers fly to heaven. Because the letters in Satan's name equal 364, the rabbis said that Satan is present 364 days a year; on Yom Kippur, however, Satan has no power over the Jewish people.

After this meal, no food or drink is consumed until after sunset the next day. This is a twenty-five-hour fast. Children under thirteen and sick adults don't have to fast, but starting at about nine years of age, some children begin to fast by skipping breakfast or waiting until two o'clock to eat lunch.

When the afternoon meal ends, the food and dishes are cleared, but the white tablecloth is left on the table. Some people set books on the table instead of plates because on Yom Kippur learning is all the nourishment that is needed. The candles are lit to begin the holiday, and the family gets ready to go to the *Kol Nidre* service at the synagogue. Some parents bless their children before they leave the house, saying these words: "May God bless you and keep you, and shine God's countenance upon you. May he make you like Ephraim and Manasseh and like Sarah, Rebecca, Rachel, and Leah." The family may also light memorial candles, called *yahrzeit* candles, to rekindle the memory of dead relatives.

The Kol Nidre service begins when the setting sun is level with the treetops. The atmosphere of the synagogue on this night is extraordinary. First of all, more people come for the Kol Nidre service than for any other service of the year. Extra chairs are brought into the main room, and special services may be scheduled for the overflow of people.

Everywhere you look, there is the color white for freshness and simplicity. The rabbi and the cantor, the singer who leads the congregation in prayer, wear white gowns to resemble the

A couple shares a tallit.   BILL ARON

kittel. The kittel is a white robe that is worn by a bridegroom, by the leader of the Passover seder, and at one's burial. It is a garment of purity and humility and is a reminder of life and death—one of the themes of the High Holy Days. The holy ark is draped with white curtains, and all the Torahs are dressed with white instead of their usual bright coverings. Even the flowers decorating the synagogue are white. Many people wear white *kippot (yarmulkes)* or head coverings out of respect for God.

Jews over thirteen wear a prayer shawl called a tallit. The tallit is a long rectangular garment with four fringes (*tzitzit*), tied into intricate knots, on each corner. In ancient times non-Jewish royalty wore fringes on the hems of their clothes to indicate their high position. The Torah instructs all Jews to remember that they are a nation of priests with God as their ruler. Most Jews today wear fringes only when they pray.

The tallit holds another meaning for the Kol Nidre service. It was the garment worn by the judges during trials in ancient times. On Yom Kippur, Jews are ending a period of judging their deeds. Because the tallit is never put on at night, the Kol Nidre service begins a little earlier than other festival evening services.

Once people arrive at the synagogue, they go to their seats. But they do not sit down. Instead they wait for the rabbi and the cantor to circle the congregation with at least two Torahs. Everyone stands in the aisles, near where the Torahs pass, to reach out and touch the Torahs with a corner of their tallit or mahzor. Then they kiss the corner of the mahzor.

When the rabbi and the cantor return to the front of the synagogue and the Torahs have been returned to the holy ark, the chanting of the Kol Nidre begins. The Kol Nidre haunts, touches, and moves Jews in an almost mystical way. More than the words, the melody possesses a power, like the shofar, to open the heart. The words are simple:

All vows and oaths we take, all promises and obligations we make to God between this Yom Kippur and the next, we hereby publicly retract in the event that we should forget them, and hereby declare our intention to be absolved of them.

The prayer, which is chanted three times by the cantor, clears the slate between each person and God: All promises that

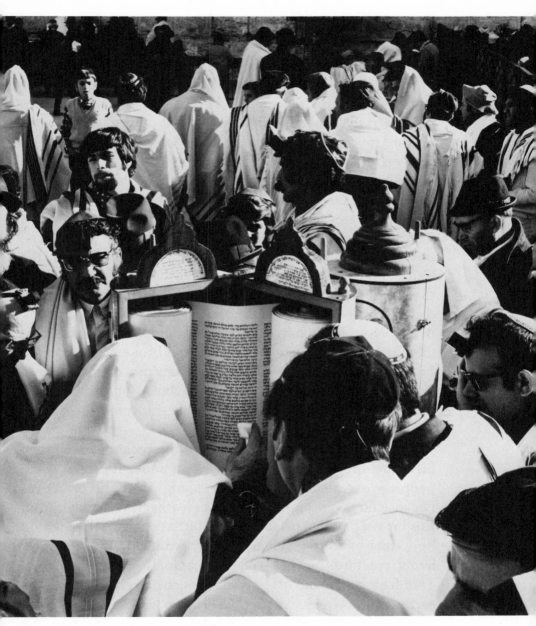

Touching the Torah with tallitzim

could not be kept during the year are now forgotten. It is time to start again. This prayer does not apply to the promises made between people, though. It only applies to the promises made between an individual and God. Promises made by one person to another can only be changed by agreement between the two people.

Unlike other prayers, which are recited in Hebrew, the more than 1,000-year-old Kol Nidre prayer is recited in Aramaic, the everyday language of the Jews in ancient times. This was so that everyone could understand the words. The prayer was especially poignant for the Spanish Jews of the fourteenth and fifteenth centuries. The Church ordered them to choose between death and becoming Christian. Many died. Others chose to live secretly as Jews but publicly took the vows of Christianity. They were called Marranos. Because they had accepted another religion and broken their bond to Judaism, they normally couldn't be considered Jews. But on Yom Kippur eve, they met to pray together. For the Marranos, Kol Nidre had special meaning because it freed them from their vows to another religion.

The next day, everyone returns to the synagogue. Usually there are special services for children under thirteen. Many people wear sneakers or sandals made of plastic or canvas because no one is supposed to wear leather on fast days. Yom Kippur is a day that celebrates the birth of a new self; it would be wrong to wear a garment made from the skin of a once-living creature. No life—plant or animal—is consumed on Yom Kippur. Taking off your shoes is also a reminder that the earth is holy. Moses removed his shoes when he spoke to God, because God said, "Put off your shoes from your feet, for the place where you stand is holy."

Fasting is not a punishment on Yom Kippur. It is a reminder

to the Jews of how dependent people are upon God and upon one another for food. The fast is also a reminder of how it feels to be hungry, and that the poor and hungry need help.

Yom Kippur prayers stress the limitations of human beings. The *Aleinu,* which is said every day of the year, includes the phrase "We bend the knee and bow." On Yom Kippur, the congregation does more than the usual bending of the knee— they put their foreheads on the ground during this prayer. For some this is humbling; they feel defenseless or like animals. For others, this posture makes them feel closer to the earth.

The prayer of confession, the *Al Het,* is repeated eight times communally and publicly. People ask to be forgiven for all wrongdoings, large and small. The word "we" is used instead of "I" because everyone makes mistakes. For example, the words are: "For the sin we have committed by disrespecting parents and teachers, for the sin we have committed by lying, and for the sin we have committed by shaming someone, for all these, O God, forgive us and pardon us." As each wrongdoing is recited, people tap their hearts gently with the closed fist of the right hand. This is done not to strike themselves, but to put themselves in touch with what they've done wrong and how they can change.

Most of the prayers are sung in Hebrew, and their melodies are hypnotic. The meaning of the words often lies beyond the words themselves. It's the repetition, the familiarity of the melodies, and the knowledge that Jews all over the world are doing the same thing, that help Jews to concentrate on this day.

The haftarah portion that is read on Yom Kippur afternoon is the story of Jonah. God asked Jonah to go to Nineveh to warn the people that if they didn't stop their idol worship, they would be destroyed. Jonah didn't want to do this task

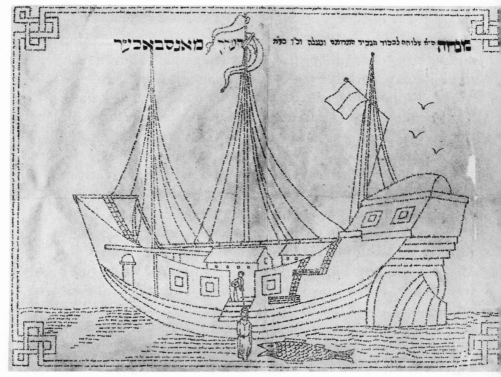

A micrography of "Jonah and the Whale." The miniature script depicts the story. Executed by Moshe Eliyahu Goldsch, 1881 JTS

because he didn't believe the people would listen to him. He tried to escape from God. He fled to a ship. When a great storm blew up at sea, the sailors feared it was because of Jonah and threw him overboard. He was swallowed by a whale and, in its belly, he prayed to God to save him. This part of the story makes it clear that there is no escaping God, just as there is no escaping your conscience.

Once again God told Jonah to go to Nineveh to deliver the holy message. Jonah went and the people listened. They fasted and prayed that they might live. When God saw this, the people of Nineveh were saved. Everyone was happy except Jonah. He didn't believe the people had really changed and he thought that they should be punished. Once again he left and found a place to rest. God provided a large gourd plant to shade Jonah, and he was happy. But the next day a worm attacked the plant and killed it. In the blazing heat, Jonah wept and told God that he wanted to die. God said, "You cared about the plant, which you did not work for and which you did not grow, which appeared overnight and died overnight. And should not I care about Nineveh, that great city, in which there are more than a hundred and twenty thousand people?" Jonah's story is a reminder that no one escapes God, since no one escapes himself. The story also celebrates teshuvah and God's forgiveness. Human beings may change, and even a prophet like Jonah cannot predict their future.

Celebration has always been part of the holiday. In ancient Jerusalem, young unmarried women danced in the vineyards with the marriageable men of the community. Many wedding dates were set on that day. The poor girls borrowed fine clothes from the wealthy girls so that there would be no difference between rich and poor. It was not a day of sadness but one of rejoicing.

In the days of the Temple, Yom Kippur was called the Great Day. Only on that day did the High Priest exchange his grand robe and gold jewelry for the simple *kittel*. During the service, he entered a small hidden room—the Holy of Holies—that was located behind the ark and was used only one day a year. This was the main event of the day. In this room the High Priest prayed to God to forgive the Jewish people. The congregation waited anxiously until the priest reappeared. Also during Yom Kippur, the High Priest spoke God's name ten times. It was never spoken by anyone else at any time. When the Temple was destroyed, the name of God was lost. *God, Jehovah, Adonai,* and *Elohim* are names used to mean the Blessed One, but they are only substitutes for the name.

The Temple was scrubbed and cleaned for Yom Kippur. When the Temple was destroyed, the external washing ended, but an inner cleansing replaced it. Each person purified himself inside and became a living sanctuary. In time it became a day on which each individual could become reborn through self-examination, confession, and correcting one's mistakes.

Many people stay in the synagogue all day on Yom Kippur, but if they have young children, they go home to give them lunch. At five o'clock everyone returns for the *Ne'ilah* (Closing the Gates) service that ends the holiday. The holy ark is left open for the service, and those who are able stand until the end of the holiday, which comes at approximately seven o'clock. A burst of energy emerges at the end of the day, even though everyone is hungry, and the year ahead feels fresh and new.

The service closes with the holiest Jewish prayer, the *Shema:* "Hear O Israel, the Lord our God, the Lord is One." The Shema ends Yom Kippur for a good reason. Some holidays have symbols that you can see, such as the Hanukkah menorah, or taste, such as the Passover matzah. But on the High Holy days, people listen: to the shofar, to the Kol Nidre, to people asking forgiveness, to themselves. And God listens to everyone's prayers. The word *shema* means "Hear!," and the Jewish people listen carefully to the words "the Lord is One."

A long steady note is blown on the shofar to signal the end of Yom Kippur. But it is really another beginning—of a new year, a renewed self, a new moon. The new moon of Tishri is blessed outdoors before the fast is broken. Then, at home, everyone joins together in a light meal. Breaking the fast with friends and family is a happy way to end the holiday. The food is light, but there is no special menu. Fruit, cheese, yogurt, and tea are often served. After the meal, many families go outside and hammer in the first post for the sukkah, the handmade shack in which they will celebrate Sukkot five days later. This connects the end of Yom Kippur, a serious fast holiday, to the beginning of Sukkot, a happy, bountiful holiday.

Apple and honey

BILL ARON

4
Apples and honey

*Eat the fat and drink the sweet . . . for this day
is holy unto the Lord.*

NEHEMIAH 8:10

The food for Rosh Hashanah is perfect for anyone who has a sweet tooth. Most of it is sweet, none of it is bitter, and the recipes have easy-to-find ingredients.

Sephardic Jews serve foods that express their wishes for the new year. The shapes, names, and parts of their food are as important as its taste. The centerpiece of a Sephardic holiday meal is a large plate that contains the following foods: apple in honey for a year as good as the apple and as sweet as the honey; a pumpkin or gourd for a year of blessing as full as the gourd; a beet to beat those who have been enemies; dates to date the year that is beginning as one of happiness, blessing, and peace for all; a leek, which is a kind of scallion, for luck that will never be lacking in the year to come; and a pomegranate for a year of good deeds as rich as the

57

pomegranate is rich with seeds. The cooked head of a sheep or fish lies on another plate. The head is a symbol for "getting ahead."

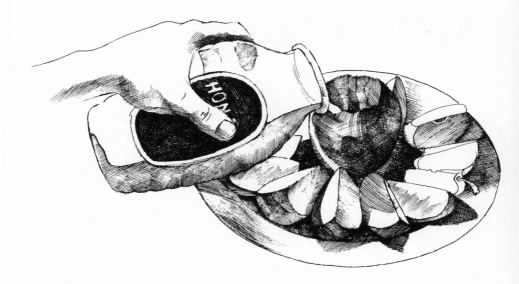

APPLES AND HONEY

This isn't really a recipe, but rather a list of instructions for serving apples and honey in a special way. Cut four apples, two red and two green or yellow, into quarters. Cut them right before you're ready to serve them, because they turn brown soon after they're sliced. Take out the seeds and remove the stems. Arrange them in alternating colors on a large plate. Place a small bowl the size of a pudding cup in the center, and fill the bowl with honey, or you can use a hollowed-out apple filled with honey instead of the bowl.

Set the plate near one person at the table so that he or she can dip the ends of the apple pieces in the honey and give them to everyone else. People will get sticky from the honey and apple juice, but that's all right. Just tell them to lick their fingers!

The following recipes require some cooking or cutting, so it's a good idea to have an adult around during the preparation and, if you're kind, for the eating of these treats.

HONEY-BAKED APPLES

6 apples
1 cup honey (¼ liter)
¼ cup orange juice (½ deciliter)
2 tablespoons lemon juice
¼ teaspoon nutmeg
heavy cream (optional)

Core the apples and put them into a baking dish. Mix the honey, orange juice, lemon juice, and nutmeg together, and pour the mixture over the apples. Bake, uncovered, at 375° F. (190° C.) for 45 minutes. While the apples are cooking, pour the surrounding liquid over them with a spoon. Remove the apples from the oven, cool them for a half-hour, and serve. They're delicious with cream poured over them, too.

HALLAH

This is the same recipe as the one for hallah eaten on the Sabbath and on festivals, but the shape of the Rosh Hashanah hallah is different.

1 cup (¼ liter) warm water (98° F. or 36.7° C.)
1 package dry yeast
2 teaspoons sugar
1½ teaspoons salt
2 tablespoons vegetable oil
2 eggs
3½ cups white flour
   (490 grams)

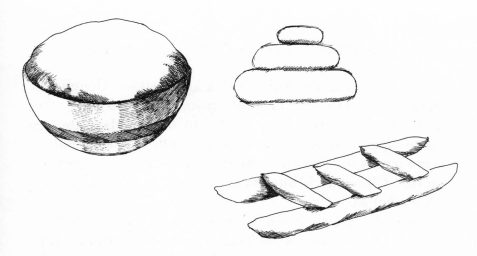

Pour a cup of warm water into a large bowl. Add the yeast and stir until it is dissolved. Add the sugar, salt, and oil, and mix until blended. Add the eggs and beat slightly until they are mixed evenly. Pour in all but a half-cup of the flour, and thoroughly stir the flour into the liquid. Sprinkle the remaining flour on a board and dump the flour mixture onto it. This is the kneading part. Rub a little flour on your hands and punch a hole in the middle of the dough. Then take the dough and fold it over the hole. Punch it down again. Repeat this punching and folding for three minutes. Then put the dough back in the mixing bowl. Cover the bowl with a damp cloth, and let the dough rise for two hours.

Flour the wooden board again and put the dough on it. It should be twice as big as it was when you first put it in the bowl. Punch it down and begin to shape it into a long snake, about 18 inches long. Place the dough on a cookie sheet. To make a crown-shaped hallah, hold one end in place and wrap the rest of the dough in a circle around it, so that the center is higher than the outer circle. It should be round and turbanlike when you're done. Separate the white from the yolk of an egg and save the yolk. Dip your fingers into the yolk and smear it over the dough. This will make the crust shiny after the hallah has baked.

You make a ladder hallah with a long snake of dough, too. Break it into thirds and put one piece aside. Take the other two pieces and lay them parallel to one another, about 6 inches apart. Break the third piece into three pieces and lay them across the first two pieces of hallah like the rungs of a ladder. Glaze the ladder with egg yolk as you did for the crown hallah.

Bake the crown hallah in a preheated oven at 350° F. (175° C.) for 45 minutes; the ladder hallah for 35 minutes. Take the baking sheet out of the oven, lift the bread off, and tap the bottom of the bread. If it sounds hollow, it's done. You can eat it right away or wait for it to cool. This bread tastes nothing like store-bought bread. It's light, sweet, and delicious.

HONEY CAKE

Honey cake is a traditional Rosh Hashanah treat. It can be made plain or with a nut-and-fruit filling.

> *4 eggs*
> *1 cup sugar (200 grams)*
> *1 cup honey*
> *¾ cup strong black instant coffee*
> *½ cup vegetable oil*
> *4 cups white flour (560 grams)*
> *7 teaspoons baking powder*
> *1½ teaspoons baking soda*
> *¼ teaspoon each cloves, nutmeg, cinnamon*
> *½ cup chopped walnuts and raisins*
> *heavy cream, whipped (optional)*

Mix the eggs and sugar together in a large bowl. Combine the honey and coffee in a small bowl. Add the oil to the sugar and

eggs, then stir in the honey and coffee. Mix together the flour,
baking powder, baking soda, spices, nuts, and raisins in a
medium-sized bowl. Add this to the mixture in the large bowl
and beat until everything is completely blended and smooth.
Line two 4½ by 8 ½-inch rectangular baking pans with aluminum foil; the foil should hang over the edges. Pour the batter
into it and bake at 350° F. (175° C.) for an hour. Let the cakes
cool for a half-hour. Then lift the foil to remove them from the
pans, and let the cakes cool for another half-hour. Honey cake

tastes fine plain, but it is delicious with whipped cream sprinkled with cinnamon on top.

TZIMMES

The word *tzimmes* in Yiddish means making a big deal out of something. The word comes from a recipe that is a mixture of many foods which cook together for hours. This tzimmes, however, is not a big deal. It uses just carrots and takes only a few minutes to cook.

1 bunch of skinny carrots
3 tablespoons vegetable oil
¼ cup water
3 tablespoons honey

Cut the carrots into round slices. Cook them for 5 minutes in a frying pan over medium heat with just enough oil to coat them. Add the water and let it simmer until the carrots are almost soft. Add the honey. If the water boils away, add a little more, simmer a minute longer, and serve.

KAYEK

Kayek are biscuits eaten by Syrian Jews to break the Yom Kippur fast.

2 cups flour (280 grams)
2 teaspoons baking powder
½ cup water
2 eggs
3 tablespoons oil
1 teaspoon salt
½ cup sesame seeds

Put the flour and baking powder in a large bowl. Make a hole in the center of the flour and place the rest of the ingredients in it. Mix everything together. The mixture will be sticky and a little dry. Put the dough on a very well floured table or cutting board. With a rolling pin, roll the dough as thin as you can. Cut it into cracker-size pieces and lift the pieces, with a spatula, onto an ungreased cookie sheet. Bake at 375° F. (190° C.) for 20 minutes.

shofar

fish

jar of honey

ladder hallah

crown hallah

mahzor

apple

שָׁנָה טוֹבָה
(Shanah Tovah)

Jonah and the whale

CRAFT DESIGNS

5
CRAFTS

*Praised are You, O Lord, for all the colors in
the rainbow, for eyes that are made for seeing
and for beauty that is its own excuse for being.*

HAROLD SCHULWEIS

Just as clocks mark the minutes and hours of the day, calendars mark the days and months of the year. Every new year, the old calendar, filled with important days from the previous year; comes down from the wall. A fresh new one, waiting for its own special days to be marked, replaces it. Making a calendar can be the first new thing you do for the new year. You can make it special by designing something fancy for your own important days, such as your birthday and favorite holidays.

Your calendar should be two calendars in one—a Jewish and a general calendar. This is less complicated than it sounds. First, find a Jewish calendar for the coming year. Some banks and kosher butchers give them away for free. The Jewish cal-

67

endar looks like an ordinary calendar except for two things. It begins in September instead of January, and it gives two dates for each day: the general date and the date according to Jewish tradition. Use this calendar as a guide for your own calendar.

Take a piece of blank paper—typing paper is good for this—and, holding it horizontally, draw a line across the page two inches from the top. Draw four more lines, 1½ inches apart, underneath. Then draw six vertical lines, 1½ inches apart, as shown in the drawing, to make thirty-five squares—seven across and five down.

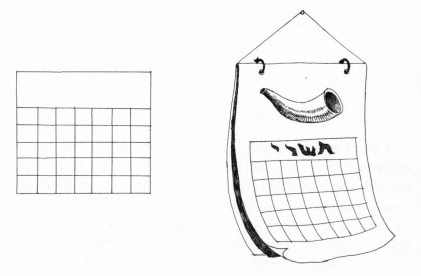

Take this page to a copying machine—most libraries and post offices have one—and make eleven copies. Beginning with September, copy the dates from the Jewish calendar onto your copies. Head each page with the month, and be sure that you mark the first of the month in the right square. Then get twelve pages of large construction paper, at least 12 inches by 18 inches, and paste the calendar onto it. Decorate the top half of the page with pictures of things that remind you of the month. You may want to leave extra space for adding things later during the month itself. Here are some picture ideas for each month.

SEPTEMBER: a shofar for Rosh Hashanah and Yom Kippur.

OCTOBER: sukkah, pumpkins and gourds for Sukkot.

NOVEMBER: turkeys and Indian corn for Thanksgiving; books for Jewish Book Month.

DECEMBER: a hanukkiyyah and a dreidel for Hanukkah.

JANUARY: a snowman or a ski scene.

FEBRUARY: a bare tree for the New Year of the Trees, Tu bi-Shevat.

MARCH: *grager* (noisemaker) and pictures of Queen Esther or Haman for Purim.

APRIL: Elijah's cup, matzot for Passover; flowers for spring.

MAY: a flag of Israel for Yom ha-Azma'ut, Israeli Independence Day.

JUNE: a tablet of the Ten Commandments for Shavuot, the festival which celebrates Moses' receiving the Law, and fruit, since it's also a harvest festival.

JULY: an American flag for the Fourth of July.

AUGUST: a tent for camping; a sailboat on a lake.

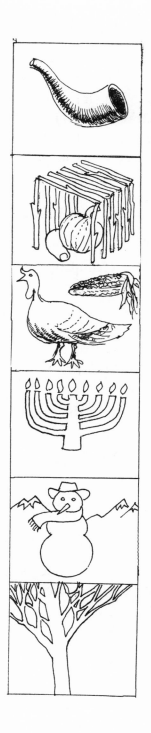

You might also include photographs of friends or relatives in their birthday months, or pictures of your favorite rock group or sports team in the months they'll be on television or in your city. Punch two holes 5 inches apart on the top of all the pages and put a piece of yarn, 12 inches long, through the holes. Tie the yarn, and hang the calendar on a nail.

The High Holy Days are a time of giving to people who need help (tzedakah). Many people contribute to charity or set time aside to help someone in need. Maybe you can babysit for a neighbor or relative with small children, or run errands for someone who is housebound.

Many families have a pretty cover for the hallah on Shabbat (the Sabbath). It is rectangular or oval to cover the Shabbat hallah. It *can* be used for the Rosh Hashanah hallah, but it won't fit very well since the holiday bread is round. Making a special Rosh Hashanah cover is another way to set the holiday apart.

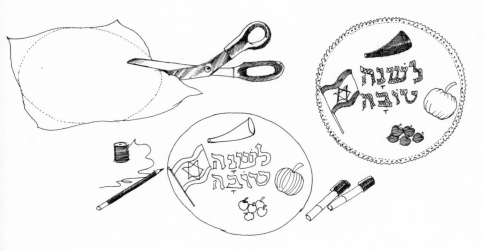

Pin a piece of paper to a piece of cotton cloth. Cut out a circle, 10 inches in diameter. Take out the pins so that you have two circles—a paper one and a cloth one. Write the Hebrew letters for *Shanah Tovah*

לְשָׁנָה טוֹבָה

in the center of the paper circle and decorate the rest of the space with the designs at the beginning of the chapter. Since this is a sample hallah cover, you can draw with a pencil. Then sew white ribbon or lace around the edges of the cotton circle. With permanent markers, copy your design from the paper circle onto the fabric circle. Be sure to put newspaper underneath the fabric to absorb the ink. Using a simple crosstitch that looks like this—xxx—embroider the designs with blue embroidery thread.

A holiday collage helps to make the house festive for the New Year. Tape together four pieces of cardboard (the kind that comes with laundered or new shirts) to make one large board. If you don't have shirt boards, you can use any stiff paper, such as oak tag, as long as it's roughly 3 feet by 2 feet. Cover the surface with aluminum foil, shiny side up. The reflection from the foil is a reminder of the High Holy Days, a time to reflect or think about deeds of the past year.

Using white glue, paste pictures that remind you of Rosh Hashanah onto the shiny surface—for example, magazine photographs of babies and newborn animals as symbols for creation and birth, cookies and cakes for sweetness, and apples and honey for a sweet, good year. Since this is a time of thoughtfulness, look for pictures of people in different moods. Rosh Hashanah is a time to look at your own moods and to think of other people's feelings, too.

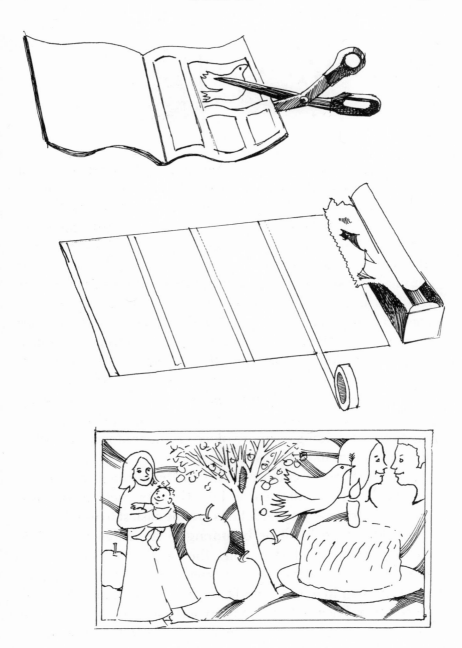

Pomander balls are not specifically Jewish, but they make a fresh pick-me-up at Yom Kippur. All you need is a lemon, ground cinnamon, and whole cloves. Use a toothpick to stick holes all over the lemon. Roll the lemon in ground cinnamon. Then put the cloves into the holes. The cloves and lemon give off a sweet fragrance that helps you to forget your hunger during the fast. Pomander balls also make nice gifts for your relatives and friends. After the holiday, cover the lemon with cheesecloth or any thin fabric and tie the corners together with a string. Hang the lemon in your room to give it a nice scent. As the lemon gradually dries out, it will become more fragrant. An orange or apple can be used instead of a lemon.

New Year cards are fun to make, and they help you keep in touch with friends and family who live far away. Make an envelope by folding a square piece of paper along the dotted lines as shown in the drawing.

Pressed flowers can be glued to the surface to make a beautiful and unusual card. Flat flowers such as pansies, honeysuckle, or even dandelions are the easiest to use. Most of these flowers will still be blooming in late August, which is when you should start making the cards. Lay the flowers, along with a few leaves from the plant, between waxed paper and put them in a heavy book, such as a telephone directory. Place several heavy books on top and leave them like this for two weeks. Gently remove the flowers from the book. They should be flat and dry, and their colors should still be vivid.

With a watercolor brush, paint the backs of the flowers with white glue. Then center the flowers on the front of the card and press lightly. After the glue is dry—in a couple of hours—open the card and write in Hebrew, "*Shanah Tovah*"

לְשָׁנָה טוֹבָה

or in English, "May you have a good and sweet year."

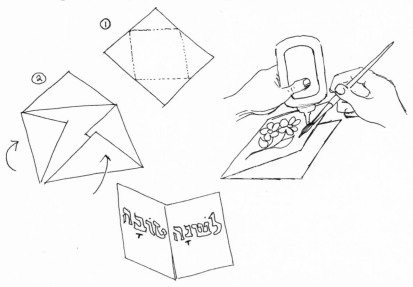

Prayer is especially important on Rosh Hashanah and Yom Kippur, but praying daily helps you to keep in touch with God all year. Observant Jews pray three times a day: when they wake up, when the sun sets, and before they go to bed. When all the Jews lived in ancient Israel, they believed they were praying in the holiest place on earth. After they were scattered across the world, they still wanted to pray in the direction of where the Temple stood, which was east. To remember which way was east, they made a decorative picture or object called a *mizrah*, which is the Hebrew word for "east."

Making a mizrah is a fine way to look forward to the new

year and to remember an old custom. It can be a painting, a plaque, a collage, or a paper-cut. There is no rule about how it should look or what it should be made from, except that pictures of people may not appear on it. This is because the second commandment forbids the copying of God's form, and a human being is made in the image of God.

Animals, flowers, and symbols, such as the menorah and star of David, are common mizrah figures. Origami paper makes an especially pretty paper-cut mizrah. Here are a few examples of symmetrical mizrahim you can make by folding a piece of colored paper in half and cutting. Paste the cut-out on a larger piece of white paper for a striking contrast. With a marking pen, write a word—

mizrah מִזְרָה   *shema* שְׁמַע

shalom שָׁלוֹם   *Adonai* יָי

or any word that has special meaning for you—across the bottom. If you're more comfortable with English, use English.

Don't forget that your mizrah must be hung on the eastern wall of your house or apartment. Even if you don't pray every day, the mizrah can be a resting place for you. You can pause in the midst of a busy day, look at it for a minute, then close your eyes and remember that you still have God all around you. Some people call this pause a meditation.

6
NEW YEAR FUN

This day is holy unto the Lord your God;
mourn not nor weep....Neither be ye grieved;
for the joy of the Lord is your strength.

NEHEMIAH 8:9–10

The High Holy Days are not meant to be sad and unpleasant, and no one expects you to spend all your time thinking about your mistakes and asking forgiveness. Here are some puzzles and brain teasers to work on during the holiday. The answers start on page 81.

STINKY PINKY

A stinky pinky is a word riddle. The answer must consist of an adjective and a noun that rhyme. For example: What is a king's land? Royal soil! If the two words of the answer have only one syllable each, the answer is called a "stink pink."

What is a stink pink for what Rosh Hashanah celebrates?

A stink pink for last Yom Kippur?

A stink pink for a tough math problem?

A stinky pinky for the ba'al teki'ah?

A stinky pinky for a beekeeper's income?

SCRAMBLED WORDS

These words have something to do with the meaning of Rosh Hashanah and Yom Kippur. Can you unscramble them?

RASFOH
TRUREN
NORFIGGVI
MUDJTENG

CODE

Here is a code that looks a little like Hebrew. See if you can break the code and decipher this Rosh Hashanah message.

‎>⅃ꓱ ꓱΛꓵ ⊏⅃◻◻ ⅃ ⌊ΛΛⵗ ⅃⸜ⵗ ⊏ⵝ◻◻⌊ ꓱ◻⅃ꓵ!

WORD COUNT

How many words can you make from the letters of these words? (Two-letter words and proper nouns are not allowed.)

Reflection
Creation
Remembrance

ANSWERS

STINKY PINKY

earth birth
past fast
brain drain
master blaster
honey money

SCRAMBLED WORDS

SHOFAR
RETURN
FORGIVING
JUDGMENT

CODE

May you have a good and sweet year!

WORD COUNT

Reflection

con	cent	lone	cleft	center
cot	cite	nice	clone	recent
eel	clef	note	creel	refine
elf	coil	reel	crone	trifle
eon	coin	rent	elect	
ere	colt	rile	enter	
fee	cone	riot	erect	conifer
fin	core	rite	fleet	elector
fir	corn	role	flier	
for	feel	rote	flint	
ice	feet	tent	relic	reflect
ion	felt	tier	rifle	election
ire	fern	tile	trice	erection
let	fete	tire		
lit	file	toil		
lot	fine	tree		
nit	fire			
nor	flee			
not	flit			
oil	foil			
one	fore			
ore	free			
rot	into			
ten	left			
tic	lift			
tin	lint			
ton	loin			

Creation

ace	net	cane	rate	antic	action
act	nit	cant	rent	crate	cantor
air	nor	care	rice	crone	cretin
ant	not	cart	riot	enact	ration
arc	oar	cent	rite	irate	recant
are	oat	cite	rote	oaten	trance
art	one	coat	tear	ocean	
ate	ore	coin	tine	ratio	
can	ran	cone	tire	react	reaction
car	rat	core	tone	tenor	
cat	roe	corn	tore	trace	
con	rot	earn		train	
cot	tan	into		trice	
ear	tar	near			
eat	tea	neat			
eon	ten	nice			
era	tic	note			
ice	tin	race			
ion	toe	rain			
ire	ton	rant			

Remembrance

ace	bare	amber	bearer	embrace
arc	barn	brace	careen	
are	beam	cream	career	
arm	bean	ember	member	remember
ban	bear			
bar	beer			
can	bran			
car	care			
ear	crab			
era	cram			
err	earn			
man	mace			
mar	mane			
men	mare			
nab	mean			
ram	mere			
ran	near			
	race			
	ream			

Appendix

HIGH HOLY DAY PRAYERS

Blessing for lighting the candles:

> Praised are You, Lord our God, Ruler of the universe, who has taught us the way of holiness through Your commandments, which include the mitzvah of kindling the [Shabbat and the] Festival lights.

Blessing over the wine (kiddush):

> Praised are You, Lord our God, King of the universe who creates fruit of the vine.
>
> Praised are You, Lord our God, King of the universe who has chosen and distinguished us by sanctifying our lives with His commandments. Lovingly have You given us [*this Shabbat and*] this Day of Remembrance, a day for [*recalling*] the shofar sound, a day for holy assembly and for recalling the Exodus from

Egypt. Thus have You chosen us, sanctifying us among all people. Your faithful word endures forever. Praised are You, Lord, King of all the earth who sanctifies [*Shabbat,*] the people Israel and the Day of Remembrance.

Blessing over food:

Praised are You, O Lord, Who gives us food from the earth.

U-NETANNEH TOKEF

How many shall leave this world and how many shall be born into it, who shall live and who shall die, who shall live out the limit of his days and who shall not, who shall perish by fire and who by water, who by sword and who by beast, who by hunger and who by thirst, who by earthquake and who by plague, who by strangling and who by stoning, who shall rest and who shall wander, who shall be at peace and who shall be tormented, who shall be poor and who shall be rich, who shall be humbled and who shall be exalted.

GLOSSARY

AL HET—Public prayer of confession.

ALEINU—A daily prayer.

ASERET YEMEI TESHUVAH—Ten Days of Teshuvah; (Days of Awe).

BA'AL TEKI'AH—Master of the shofar; shofar blower.

BA'AL TESHUVAH—Master of the return; person who goes through teshuvah.

ELUL—Hebrew month of preparation before Rosh Hashanah.

HALLAH (hallot, pl.)—Holiday bread.

HA-MOTZI—Blessing said over food.

KAPPAROT—Ceremony the day before Yom Kippur which expresses the idea of getting rid of old, worn-out habits.

KIBBUTZ (kibbutzim, pl.)—Community in Israel where people live, work, and eat together.

KIDDUSH—Sanctification over wine of the Sabbath and the festivals.

KIPPAH (kippot, pl.)—Special head covering worn during prayer; yarmulke.

KITTEL—White gown worn on Yom Kippur, at the Passover seder, by the bridegroom at his wedding, and at burial. A garment of purity and humility, and to remind one of life and death.

KOL NIDRE—Prayer said on the holiest night of the year, the eve of Yom Kippur; literally means "All Vows."

MAHZOR—High Holy Day prayer book containing prayers, songs, and commentary.

MIDRASH—Story or legend that has its beginnings in the Torah; often it explains some part of the Torah.

MITZVAH (mitzvot, pl.)—Good deed; rule or commandment that Jews believe God gave them to lead a good life.

MIZRAH (mizrahim, pl.)—Decorative plaque placed on the eastern wall in traditional Jewish homes.

NE'ILAH—Last service on Yom Kippur; closing.

ROSH HASHANAH—Head of the Year; New Year.

ROSH HODESH—Head of the Month; New Moon.

SELIHA (selihot, pl.)—Special night prayer chanted before the High Holy Days; penitential prayer.

SHABBAT SHUVAH—Sabbath of the Return; the Sabbath that falls between Rosh Hashanah and Yom Kippur.

SHAMMASH—Caretaker of the synagogue.

SHE-HEHEYANU—Prayer of thanksgiving.

SHEMA—Holiest Jewish prayer.

SHEVARIM—Three short blasts blown on the shofar during Rosh Hashanah.

SHOFAR (shofarot, pl.)—Trumpet made from a ram's horn or any kosher animal and blown during the High Holy Days.

SUKKOT—Harvest holiday that follows five days after Yom Kippur.

TALLIT—Prayer shawl.

TALMUD—Body of Jewish civil and ceremonial law.

TASHLIKH—Ceremony of the casting away of sins.

TEFILLAH—Prayer.

TEKI'AH—Long, clear blast blown on the shofar during Rosh Hashanah.

TEKI'AH GEDOLAH—Final, long blast blown on the shofar at the end of Rosh Hashanah and Yom Kippur.

TERU'AH—Nine very fast, short blasts blown on the shofar during Rosh Hashanah.

TESHUVAH—Returning to God; self-examination.

TISHRI—Hebrew month in which Rosh Hashanah and Yom Kippur fall.

TORAH—The first five books of the Bible; guidance, direction.

TZEDAKAH—Giving to those in need; justice.

TZIMMES (Yiddish)—Making a "big deal" out of something; a carrot dish.

TZITZIT—Fringes on the edges of a tallit.

U-NETANNEH TOKEF—"Let Us Rehearse the Grandeur"; High Holy Day prayer which proclaims the sovereignty of God.

YAHRZEIT (Yiddish)—Anniversary of a death.

YAMIM NORA'IM—Days of Awe; the ten days between Rosh Hashanah and Yom Kippur.

YARMULKE—Special head covering worn during prayer; kippah.

YOM HA-DIN—Day of Judgment. Another name for Rosh Hashanah.

YOM HARAT OLAM—Birthday of the World.

YOM KIPPUR—Day of Cleansing, Purification; Day of Atonement.

YOM TERU'AH—Day of the Shofar.

SUGGESTED READING

S. V. Agnon, *Days of Awe* (Schocken Books, New York, 1965)

Theodore Gaster, *Festivals of the Year* (William Morrow & Co., Inc., New York, 1972)

Philip Goodman, *The Rosh Hashanah Anthology* (The Jewish Publication Society of America, Philadelphia, 1970)

Philip Goodman, *The Yom Kippur Anthology* (The Jewish Publication Society of America, 1971)

Howard Greenfeld, *Rosh Hashanah and Yom Kippur* (Holt, Rinehart, and Winston, Inc., New York, 1980)

Jules Harlow, ed., *Mahzor for Rosh Hashanah and Yom Kippur* (Rabbinical Assembly, New York, 1972)

Hayyim Schauss, *The Jewish Festivals* (Schocken Books, 1978)

Richard Siegel, *The First Jewish Catalog* (The Jewish Publication Society of America, 1973)

INDEX

93

Temple Israel

Minneapolis, Minnesota

In Honor of the Bar Mitzvah of
BILL WOLFSON
BY
Fremajane, Blair & Robby Wolfson
December 10, 1983